WORKBOOK TO
TAKE CHARGE OF YOUR CREDIT

BY CHARLISE R. RICE

A STEP-BY-STEP WORKBOOK TO REPAIRING YOUR CREDIT

AUTHOR & MERCH WEBSITE HTTPS://WWW.CHARLISERICE.COM
PROFESSIONAL RESOURCE CONSULTANT WEBSITE
HTTPS://WWW.LISESBUSINESS.COM

PRINTED IN THE UNITED STATES OF AMERICA WORKBOOK ISBN 979-8-9879207-3-2, TAKE CHARGE OF YOUR CREDIT 979-8-9879207-4-9. BOOK AND WORKBOOK PACKAGE 979-8-9879207-5-6
DISCLAIMER AND/OR LEGAL NOTICES: THE INFORMATION PRESENTED HEREIN REPRESENTS THE VIEW OF THE AUTHOR AS OF THE DATE OF PUBLICATION. BECAUSE OF THE RATE WITH WHICH CONDITIONS CHANGE, THE AUTHOR RESERVES THE RIGHT TO ALTER AND UPDATE HER OPINION BASED ON THE NEW CONDITIONS. THE REPORT IS FOR INFORMATIONAL PURPOSES ONLY. WHILE EVERY ATTEMPT HAS BEEN MADE TO VERIFY THE INFORMATION PROVIDED IN THIS BOOK, NEITHER THE AUTHOR ASSUMES ANY RESPONSIBILITY FOR ERRORS, INACCURACIES, OR OMISSIONS. ANY SLIGHTS OF PEOPLE OR ORGANIZATIONS ARE UNINTENTIONAL. IF ADVICE CONCERNING LEGAL OR RELATED MATTERS IS NEEDED, THE SERVICES OF A FULLY QUALIFIED PROFESSIONAL SHOULD BE SOUGHT. THIS BOOK IS NOT INTENDED FOR USE AS A SOURCE OF LEGAL OR ACCOUNTING ADVICE. YOU SHOULD BE AWARE OF ANY LAWS WHICH GOVERN BUSINESS TRANSACTIONS OR OTHER BUSINESS PRACTICES IN YOUR COUNTRY AND STATE. ANY REFERENCE TO ANY PERSON OR BUSINESS WHETHER LIVING OR DEAD IS PURELY COINCIDENTAL.

TABLE OF CONTENTS

ACKNOWLEDGMENTS

Thanks to my husband, DeShaun Walker, for always encouraging me, listening to my ideas, and helping me with proofreading.

Thank you God Almighty, Holy Spirit for giving me the knowledge to create this workbook and the strength to finish it.

Knowledge is powerful but sharing knowledge is empowerment-Charlise

INTRODUCTION

Repairing your credit involves several steps, including getting your credit report, budgeting, filing disputes, monitoring for fraudulent activity, contacting creditors, following up with credit bureaus, and more. I have created worksheets in this workbook to help you sort, track, and follow up (if necessary). I have gathered relevant information, such as websites, phone numbers, sample letters, and more references. My goal is to help you create an action plan and execute it.

As you go through the process of improving your credit, use these worksheets to go through the steps along with my book, Take Charge of Your Credit: A Step-by-Step Guide to Repairing Your Credit ©. These worksheets and information I designed to help you maximize your awareness, organize your steps, mark off your actions, and follow up if necessary.

If you or someone you know, 16 years old and up, need to learn the basics of credit, register for my self-paced workshop, Educational Credit Literacy eLearning Workshop. Scan the QR code to register.

Create a Goal, Plan, & Budget

CREATE A GOAL, PLAN, & BUDGET

You have gotten this far because you want to do better with your credit. It is best to create a goal, plan, and budget. I tell people all the time to write down their goals, and what they want to accomplish. Also, write down your objectives, and how you are going to get them done. Once you start working on your plan, you can check off what you accomplished.

Credit is essential to financial stability and your way of living. Your credit is checked for financing a car, renting an apartment, buying a house, renting a car, utilities, and in certain positions for employment purposes. Credit repair is NOT an overnight process or a secret magical letter that removes everything. This takes time and strategy. If you are willing to fight for your credit, this will be worth your time and effort.

I have created Goal sheets & Budget sheets for you as a guide. The Financial Goal Sheet helps you prepare the plan. Budgeting helps with creating healthy financial behaviors. This helps you effectively manage your finances. If you do not know your monthly budget, I included weekly budget sheets to help you figure this out. You may be surprised as you may need to adjust your budget to help you meet your financial goals. If your income is more than your expenses, you have money left for a savings account, emergency fund, or to resolve some of your debt. If your expenses are more than your income, then look at your budget to find what expenses are *not* a necessity to cut out or cut down on.

CREATE A GOAL, PLAN, & BUDGET

When you have figured out your budget try to stick to it as close as you can. I do understand emergencies may evolve but having an emergency plan can be a part of your budget. If you haven't already, refer to the section on Healthy Financial Behaviors in my book.

All the work you do to fix your credit is worthless if you continue to incorporate bad financial habits. Do not fix your credit for a temporary situation. For example, only fixing your credit to get a car, then after you get the car, you return to the same unhealthy financial behaviors. This entire process is meant to help you create discipline.

Be determined and create a discipline. You can do whatever it is in your heart to do. Create your discipline to change the trajectory of your credit situation. Trust the process as it will all be worth it!!

FINANCIAL GOALS

FINANCIAL GOAL

TIME FRAME

STEPS TO TAKE

FINANCIAL GOAL

TIME FRAME

STEPS TO TAKE

FINANCIAL GOALS

FINANCIAL GOAL

TIME FRAME

STEPS TO TAKE

FINANCIAL GOAL

TIME FRAME

STEPS TO TAKE

FINANCIAL GOALS

FINANCIAL GOAL

TIME FRAME

STEPS TO TAKE

FINANCIAL GOAL

TIME FRAME

STEPS TO TAKE

Weekly Budget

Expense	SUN	MON	TUES	WED	THURS	FRI	SAT
Rent/Mortg.							
Car Note							
Gas							
Cellphone							
Groceries							
Utility bills							
Insurances							
Internet							
Tithes Donations							
Childcare							
Pet Care							
TOTALS							

Weekly Budget

Week of	
Income	

Budget

Expense	SUN	MON	TUES	WED	THURS	FRI	SAT
Rent/Mortg.							
Car Note							
Gas							
Cellphone							
Groceries							
Utility bills							
Insurances							
Internet							
Tithes Donations							
Childcare							
Pet Care							
TOTALS							

Weekly Budget

Week of		Budget
Income		

Expense	SUN	MON	TUES	WED	THURS	FRI	SAT
Rent/Mortg.							
Car Note							
Gas							
Cellphone							
Groceries							
Utility bills							
Insurances							
Internet							
Tithes Donations							
Childcare							
Pet Care							
TOTALS							

Weekly Budget

| Week of | |
| Income | |

| Budget |
| |

Expense	SUN	MON	TUES	WED	THURS	FRI	SAT
Rent/Mortg.							
Car Note							
Gas							
Cellphone							
Groceries							
Utility bills							
Insurances							
Internet							
Tithes Donations							
Childcare							
Pet Care							
TOTALS							

MONTHLY BUDGET

GOAL		
INCOME -1		
INCOME -2		
OTHER INCOME		
	TOTAL INCOME	

EXPENSES
MONTH
BUDGET

BILL TO BE PAID	DUE DATE	AMOUNT	PAID

MONTHLY SUMMARY

TOTAL INCOME	TOTAL EXPENSES	DIFFERENCE

NOTES

MONTHLY BUDGET

GOAL

INCOME -1		
INCOME -2		
OTHER INCOME		
	TOTAL INCOME	

EXPENSES

MONTH
BUDGET

BILL TO BE PAID	DUE DATE	AMOUNT	PAID

MONTHLY SUMMARY

TOTAL INCOME	TOTAL EXPENSES	DIFFERENCE

NOTES

MONTHLY BUDGET

GOAL		
INCOME -1		
INCOME -2		
OTHER INCOME		
	TOTAL INCOME	

EXPENSES
MONTH
BUDGET

BILL TO BE PAID	DUE DATE	AMOUNT	PAID

MONTHLY SUMMARY

TOTAL INCOME	TOTAL EXPENSES	DIFFERENCE

NOTES

MONTHLY BUDGET

GOAL		
INCOME -1		
INCOME -2		
OTHER INCOME		
	TOTAL INCOME	

EXPENSES
MONTH
BUDGET

BILL TO BE PAID	DUE DATE	AMOUNT	PAID

MONTHLY SUMMARY

TOTAL INCOME	TOTAL EXPENSES	DIFFERENCE

NOTES

Examine Your Credit Report

Order Your Credit Report

Order from the 3 Major Credit Bureaus
-Equifax, Experian, Transunion-
Go online or call. Calling or going online to Annual Credit Report should take care of all 3 major bureaus.

Online

www.AnnualCreditReport.com

Call

Annual Credit Report 1-877-322-8288

TransUnion 1-800-916-8800
Equifax 1-800-685-1111
Experian 1-888-397-3742

Date
Ordered/
Received

Note: If you cannot get through the online steps fully, they will give you a form to mail in.

 # What to look for when examining your credit report

1. Incorrect personal information. For instance, your name is spelled wrong, incorrect addresses. This information can be linked to identity theft.
2. Accounts you do not recognize. Again, this could be identity theft and fraud.
3. Account details such as the balances, incorrect credit limits, and dates. Make sure these are correct. Also, check if accounts that you know YOU closed have actually been closed. Has to state that it was closed by the consumer.
4. Duplicate accounts such as two credit accounts with the same information. Or two different credit agencies collecting on the same account.
5. Excessive inquiries not caused by you. Could be an indicator of fraud.
6. Anything that is questionable, errors, conflicting, or inaccurate.
7. Items past the statute of limitations; Inquiries more than 2 years; Bankruptcies older than 10 years. Lawsuits, judgments, tax liens, criminal records, and or delinquent accounts for more than 7 years.

After you have examined your credit report and listed all the errors, inaccuracies, etc., it is time to tackle these issues. Time to sort out and start your plan of action. Part of your plan will enforce your objectives to take charge of your credit.

Examine Your Credit Report
LIST ACCOUNTS WITH ERRORS

ACCOUNT/CREDITOR _____

CREDIT BUREAU(S)
REPORTED ON _____

ERROR(S) _____

_____

DATE DISPUTED ____ / ____ / ____

- -

ACCOUNT/CREDITOR _____

CREDIT BUREAU(S)
REPORTED ON _____

ERROR(S) _____

_____

DATE DISPUTED ____ / ____ / ____

LIST ACCOUNTS WITH ERRORS

ACCOUNT/CREDITOR

_____

CREDIT BUREAU(S)
REPORTED ON

_____

ERROR(S)

_____

_____

DATE DISPUTED _____/_____/_____

- -

ACCOUNT/CREDITOR

_____

CREDIT BUREAU(S)
REPORTED ON

_____

ERROR(S)

_____

_____

DATE DISPUTED _____/_____/_____

LIST ACCOUNTS WITH ERRORS

ACCOUNT/CREDITOR   _____

CREDIT BUREAU(S)
REPORTED ON   _____

ERROR(S)   _____

_____

DATE DISPUTED   _____ / ____ / _____

- -

ACCOUNT/CREDITOR   _____

CREDIT BUREAU(S)
REPORTED ON   _____

ERROR(S)   _____

_____

DATE DISPUTED   _____ / ____ / _____

LIST ACCOUNTS WITH ERRORS

ACCOUNT/CREDITOR _____

CREDIT BUREAU(S)
REPORTED ON _____

ERROR(S) _____

_____

DATE DISPUTED ____ / ____ / ____

- -

ACCOUNT/CREDITOR _____

CREDIT BUREAU(S)
REPORTED ON _____

ERROR(S) _____

_____

DATE DISPUTED ____ / ____ / ____

LIST ACCOUNTS WITH ERRORS

ACCOUNT/CREDITOR _____

CREDIT BUREAU(S)
REPORTED ON _____

ERROR(S) _____

_____

DATE DISPUTED _____/_____/_____

- -

ACCOUNT/CREDITOR _____

CREDIT BUREAU(S)
REPORTED ON _____

ERROR(S) _____

_____

DATE DISPUTED _____/_____/_____

Sample Dispute Letter
From FTC Consumer Information

 <u>KEEP COPIES OF EVERYTHING YOU MAIL OR EMAIL</u>

[Date]

[Your Name]

[Your Address][Your City, State, Zip Code]

[Business Name]

[Street Address][City, State, Zip Code]

Subject: Disputing Information in Credit Report

I am writing to dispute the following information that your company supplied to [give the name of the credit bureau whose report has incorrect information]. I have circled the items I dispute on the attached copy of my credit report(s).

This item [for instance: retailer account at ABC Department Store and the account number] is inaccurate [or incomplete] because [describe in detail what is inaccurate or incomplete and why] I am requesting that [business name] have the item removed [or request another specific change to correct the information.]

[Add a list and description of other disputed items, if that applies.]

Enclosed are copies of [my credit report and any other documents enclosed with a short description, for instance, your record of payments made] supporting my request. Please reinvestigate this matter and contact the national credit bureaus to have them delete [or correct] the disputed item(s) as soon as possible.

Sincerely,

[Your name]

Enclosures: [List what you are enclosing]

 IF YOU ARE MAILING YOUR LETTERS, I SUGGEST USING THE USPS FLAT RATE ENVELOPE (RED ONE). THIS IS CHEAPER THAN CERTIFIED MAIL. FLAT RATE IS INSURED AND YOU WILL RECEIVE A TRACKING NUMBER.

Fraud & Identity Theft

Report Fraud and Identity Theft IMMEDIATELY!! Freeze accounts!!

You have specific rights under the Fair Credit Reporting Act (FCRA). These rights include:

- Placing fraud alerts with the three major credit bureaus.
- Placing a security freeze on your credit report.
- Obtaining documents related to fraudulent transactions or accounts opened using your personal information.
- Obtaining information from debt collectors.
- Blocking the reporting of damaging information to the Credit Bureaus so it does not appear on your credit reports.
- Stopping businesses from reporting inaccurate information to the credit bureaus.

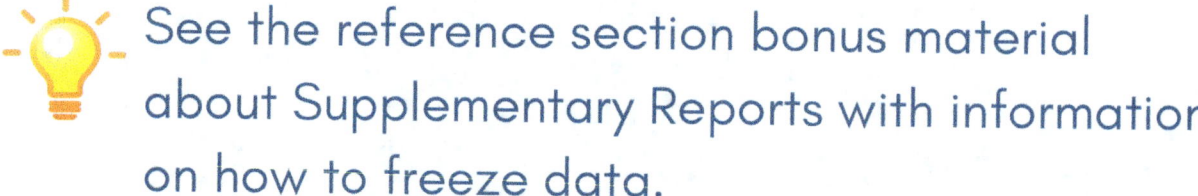 See the reference section bonus material about Supplementary Reports with information on how to freeze data.

 # FRAUD & IDENTITY THEFT
STEPS TO TAKE

1. Notify the company or agency that issued your stolen credentials.
2. Place a freeze or fraud alert on your credit.
3. Report the theft to the Federal Trade Commission.
4. File a police report with your local law enforcement agency.
5. Obtain copies of documents used to open accounts or make fraudulent transactions.
6. Change your passwords.

To report Identity Theft, place a Freeze, or Fraud Alert, place a call to one of the 3 credit bureaus. You only need to contact one of the three agencies because the law requires the agency you call to contact the other two. You can do this online too, but I suggest giving them a call as this is a serious matter.

Equifax: 1-800-525-6285; www.equifax.com
Experian: 1-888-397-3742; www.experian.com
TransUnion: 1-800-680-7289; www.transunion.com

Report identity (ID) theft to the Federal Trade Commission (FTC) online at IdentityTheft.gov or by phone at 1-877-438-4338.

An additional step you can take to help prevent Fraud and Identity theft is to sign up for Credit Monitoring. With active credit monitoring, you will receive alerts for suspicious activity such as new credit inquiries, new loans, and delinquent accounts reported in your name. Also, you receive identity theft protection with benefits that include monitoring for using your social security number, dark web monitoring, enhanced change of address notifications, and searching national and international criminal record databases for identity thieves committing crimes in your name. Also, get ID Theft Insurance. Try MyScoreIQ, usually a $1 to start.

Accounts That Are NOT Mine

LIST ACCOUNTS

ACCOUNT/CREDITOR _____

REPORTED TO
EQ, TU, EX _____ / _____ / _____

REPORTED
TO FTC _____ / _____ / _____

> **IF CALLED**
>
> SPOKE WITH _____
>
> TIME _____ AM
> PM

- -

ACCOUNT/CREDITOR _____

REPORTED TO
EQ, TU, EX _____ / _____ / _____

REPORTED TO
FTC _____ / _____ / _____

> **IF CALLED**
>
> SPOKE WITH _____
>
> TIME _____ AM
> PM

Accounts That Are NOT Mine

LIST ACCOUNTS

ACCOUNT/CREDITOR _____

REPORTED TO
EQ, TU, EX _____ / ___ / _____

REPORTED
TO FTC _____ / ___ / _____

IF CALLED

SPOKE WITH _____

TIME _____ AM
PM

- -

ACCOUNT/CREDITOR _____

REPORTED TO
EQ, TU, EX _____ / ___ / _____

REPORTED TO
FTC _____ / ___ / _____

IF CALLED

SPOKE WITH _____

TIME _____ AM
PM

Accounts That Are NOT Mine

LIST ACCOUNTS

ACCOUNT/CREDITOR _____

REPORTED TO
EQ, TU, EX _____ / _____ / _____

REPORTED
TO FTC _____ / _____ / _____

- -

ACCOUNT/CREDITOR _____

REPORTED TO
EQ, TU, EX _____ / _____ / _____

REPORTED TO
FTC _____ / _____ / _____

Accounts That Are NOT Mine

LIST ACCOUNTS

ACCOUNT/CREDITOR _____

REPORTED TO
EQ, TU, EX _____/_____/_____

REPORTED
TO FTC _____/_____/_____

IF CALLED

SPOKE WITH _____

TIME _____ AM
PM

- -

ACCOUNT/CREDITOR _____

REPORTED TO
EQ, TU, EX _____/_____/_____

REPORTED TO
FTC _____/_____/_____

IF CALLED

SPOKE WITH _____

TIME _____ AM
PM

Accounts That Are NOT Mine

LIST ACCOUNTS

ACCOUNT/CREDITOR _____

REPORTED TO
EQ, TU, EX _____ / _____ / _____

REPORTED
TO FTC _____ / _____ / _____

IF CALLED

SPOKE WITH _____

TIME _____ AM
PM

- -

ACCOUNT/CREDITOR _____

REPORTED TO
EQ, TU, EX _____ / _____ / _____

REPORTED TO
FTC _____ / _____ / _____

IF CALLED

SPOKE WITH _____

TIME _____ AM
PM

Past Due Accounts ≤ 180 days

Past Due Accounts:
Less than or about 180 days

The biggest factor in your credit score is your payment history, making up 35%.

Remember the objective here is to get your accounts paid and current as well as avoid getting charged off. Hence the plan, goal, and budget you created. The extra money you have can help you get caught up or settle some debt. Ask them what they can do to help you get current without closing your account. Also, ask if they can remove some late fees. If you do not ask, you will not know. If we are still under a COVID National Emergency Period while you are reading this, many creditors are willing to work something out.

Past Due Accounts: 120-180 days

 AVOID BEING CHARGED OFF

ASK TO DISMISS SOME LATE FEES

ACCOUNT/CREDITOR _____

DATE ____ / ____ / ____

OUTCOME/TERMS _____

_____

_____

> ### WHEN CALLED
>
> SPOKE WITH _____
>
> TIME _____ AM PM

- -

ACCOUNT/CREDITOR _____

DATE ____ / ____ / ____

OUTCOME/TERMS _____

_____

_____

> ### WHEN CALLED
>
> SPOKE WITH _____
>
> TIME _____ AM PM

Past Due Accounts: 120-180 days

 AVOID BEING CHARGED OFF

ASK TO DISMISS SOME LATE FEES

ACCOUNT/CREDITOR _____

DATE ____ / ____ / ____

OUTCOME/TERMS _____

_____

WHEN CALLED

SPOKE WITH _____

TIME _____   AM   PM

- -

ACCOUNT/CREDITOR _____

DATE ____ / ____ / ____

OUTCOME/TERMS _____

_____

WHEN CALLED

SPOKE WITH _____

TIME _____   AM   PM

Past Due Accounts: 120-180 days

 AVOID BEING CHARGED OFF

ASK TO DISMISS SOME LATE FEES

ACCOUNT/CREDITOR _____

DATE ____ / ____ / ____

WHEN CALLED

OUTCOME/TERMS _____

_____

_____

SPOKE WITH _____

TIME _____ AM / PM

- -

ACCOUNT/CREDITOR _____

DATE ____ / ____ / ____

WHEN CALLED

OUTCOME/TERMS _____

_____

_____

SPOKE WITH _____

TIME _____ AM / PM

Past Due Accounts: 120-180 days

 AVOID BEING CHARGED OFF

ASK TO DISMISS SOME LATE FEES

ACCOUNT/CREDITOR _____

DATE ____ / ____ / ____

OUTCOME/TERMS _____

_____

_____

> **WHEN CALLED**
>
> SPOKE WITH _____
>
> TIME _____ AM PM

- -

ACCOUNT/CREDITOR _____

DATE ____ / ____ / ____

OUTCOME/TERMS _____

_____

_____

> **WHEN CALLED**
>
> SPOKE WITH _____
>
> TIME _____ AM PM

Past Due Accounts: 120-180 days

 AVOID BEING CHARGED OFF

ASK TO DISMISS SOME LATE FEES

ACCOUNT/CREDITOR _____

DATE _____ / ___ / _____

OUTCOME/TERMS _____

_____

_____

> ### WHEN CALLED
>
> SPOKE WITH _____
>
> TIME _____ AM PM

- -

ACCOUNT/CREDITOR _____

DATE _____ / ___ / _____

OUTCOME/TERMS _____

_____

_____

> ### WHEN CALLED
>
> SPOKE WITH _____
>
> TIME _____ AM PM

Past Due Accounts:
Information about Charge Offs

Charge-off typically appears after six consecutive months of score reductions due to missed payments.

Charge-offs do not end your obligation to repay the debt. Check with the original creditor to see if you can still pay them directly.

If the original creditor no longer owns the account, you will owe the debt to the collection agency that acquired it. Charge-offs and other negative account history, such as late or missed payments, can stay on your credit reports for up to seven years. Charge offs and collections on your credit report projects as a risk to some lenders when it comes to issuing you loans, services, or credit.

If a charge-off is reported inaccurately, or if it fails to "fall off" your credit report after seven years, you can file a dispute with the credit bureaus to have it removed from your credit reports.

Past Due Accounts Collections

Three things to remember from my book about collections before taking these steps:

- Look at the credit removal dates.
- Request validation first!
- Do not admit to the debt.

Requesting validation is disputed under FDCPA Section 809. If you dispute any items on your credit report, Federal Law states that the credit bureau then investigate your claim and if there is an error, correct it or remove it. The key is when you dispute the items, you must tell them **what is wrong and the action** to take. There are many validation letters on the internet. The key is also to **personalize it to your situation.** The strategy is to create a paper trail, so keep any copies you send and receive. If you are mailing, I inform my clients when sending a letter, and provide a legible copy of your ID and a copy of a current bill. This will prevent delays in going back and forth because they have to verify who you are. If you do not have a current bill get an affidavit of residency. I am a Notary Public, I can also notarize this, remotely, for a fee no matter where you live. If you are mailing your letters, I suggest using USPS Flat Rate Envelope (Red one). This is cheaper than certified mail. Flat Rate is insured and you will receive a tracking number.

Under the Fair Debt Collection Practices Act (FDCPA), a debt collector must respond to a request for a debt validation letter. If they do not, they violate the act. Write to the credit bureaus to remove this debt immediately if they can't validate it. Send them copies of what you already sent so that you have proof you did your part.

You can report them to your state's attorney general, the Federal Trade Commission (FTC), or the Consumer Financial Protection Bureau (CFPB). You can also sue for up to $1,000. You would have up to one year after the incident to sue.

If you choose to negotiate and settle know this. You may face a tax burden if you do reach a settlement. If at least $600 in debt is forgiven, you will likely pay income taxes on the forgiven amount. They will send you a 1099-C. This is a cancellation of debt that you will have to file with your taxes. Speak to a tax professional about the 1099-C.

YOUR NAME
YOUR ADDRESS

CREDITOR NAME
ADDRESS

DATE

RE: VALIDATION REQUIRED /ACCT XXXXX, LAST 4 SSN XXXX

TO WHOM IT MAY CONCERN,

I RECENTLY PULLED MY CREDIT REPORT AND NOTICED YOUR ACCOUNT. I AM REQUESTING VALIDATION PURSUANT TO THE FAIR DEBT COLLECTION PRACTICES ACT, 15 U.S.C 1692G SEC. 809 (8) (FDCPA).

• PROVIDE BREAKDOWN OF FEES INCLUDING HOW YOU CALCULATED WHAT YOU CLAIM I OWE.
• IF THERE HAVE BEEN ANY OTHER CHANGES OR ADJUSTMENTS SINCE THE LAST BILLING STATEMENT FROM THE ORIGINAL CREDITOR, PLEASE PROVIDE FULL VERIFICATION AND DOCUMENTATION OF THE AMOUNT YOU ARE TRYING TO COLLECT. EXPLAIN HOW THAT AMOUNT WAS CALCULATED.
• TELL ME WHEN THE CREDITOR CLAIMS THIS DEBT BECAME DUE AND WHEN IT BECAME DELINQUENT.
• IDENTIFY THE DATE OF THE LAST PAYMENT MADE ON THIS ACCOUNT.
• CEASE ANY CREDIT BUREAU REPORTING UNTIL DEBT HAS BEEN VALIDATED BY ME AS REQUIRED UNDER THE FCRA.
SEND THIS INFORMATION TO MY ADDRESS LISTED ABOVE AND ACCEPT THIS LETTER SENT AS MY FORMAL DEBT VALIDATION REQUEST, WHICH I AM ALLOWED UNDER THE FDCPA. I HAVE ENCLOSED A COPY OF MY DRIVER'S LICENSE & MY CURRENT UTILITY BILL FOR YOUR VERIFICATION PURPOSES. I AM OPEN TO COMMUNICATING WITH YOU FOR THIS PURPOSE. PLEASE TREAT THIS DEBT AS BEING IN DISPUTE AND UNDER DISCUSSION BETWEEN US. SINCERELY,

----

YOUR NAME

IF YOU ARE MAILING YOUR LETTERS, I SUGGEST USING USPS FLAT RATE ENVELOPE (RED ONE). THIS IS CHEAPER THAN CERTIFIED MAIL. FLAT RATE IS INSURED, AND YOU WILL RECEIVE A TRACKING NUMBER.

Past Due Accounts: Collections

 DO NOT ADMIT TO THE DEBT

ACCOUNT/CREDITOR _____

ORIGINAL CREDITOR _____

REMOVAL DATE _____/_____/_____

☐ REQUEST VALIDATION

DATE _____/_____/_____

☐ FLAT RATE MAIL

☐ CALLED ➡

DID YOU RECEIVE VALIDATION WITHIN 30 DAYS?

☐ **YES**   ☐ **NO**

IF NO, CALL BACK OR SEND ANOTHER LETTER FOR IMMEDIATE REMOVAL.

IF YES, REVIEW INFORMATION AND EXAMINE TO MAKE SURE IT IS YOURS. IF NOT YOURS GO BACK TO DISPUTE STEPS AND FRAUD.

IF CALLED

SPOKE WITH _____

TIME _____ AM
PM

DURING LISTEN DID THEY...

☐ STATE MINI-MIRANDA?

☐ VERIFY YOU?

IF THE DEBT COLLECTOR DID NOT DO EITHER OF THOSE STEPS PRIOR TO SPEAKING ABOUT YOUR DEBT, HANG UP, REPORT IT TO CFPB, FTC

Past Due Accounts: Collections

 DO NOT ADMIT TO THE DEBT

ACCOUNT/CREDITOR _____

ORIGINAL CREDITOR _____

REMOVAL DATE ____/____/____

☐ REQUEST VALIDATION

DATE ____/____/____

☐ FLAT RATE MAIL

☐ CALLED ➡️

DID YOU RECEIVE VALIDATION WITHIN 30 DAYS?

☐ **YES**   ☐ **NO**

IF NO, CALL BACK OR SEND ANOTHER LETTER FOR IMMEDIATE REMOVAL.

IF YES, REVIEW INFORMATION AND XAMINE TO MAKE SURE IT IS YOURS. IF OT YOURS GO BACK TO DISPUTE STEPS AND FRAUD.

IF CALLED

SPOKE WITH _____

TIME _____   AM
                       PM

DURING LISTEN
DID THEY...

☐ STATE MINI-MIRANDA?

☐ VERIFY YOU?

IF THE DEBT COLLECTOR DID NOT DO EITHER OF THOSE STEPS PRIOR TO SPEAKING ABOUT YOUR DEBT, HANG UP, REPORT IT TO CFPB, FTC

Past Due Accounts: Collections

 DO NOT ADMIT TO THE DEBT

ACCOUNT/CREDITOR _____

ORIGINAL CREDITOR _____

REMOVAL DATE _____ / _____ / _____

☐ REQUEST VALIDATION

DATE _____ / _____ / _____

☐ FLAT RATE MAIL

☐ CALLED ➡

DID YOU RECEIVE VALIDATION WITHIN 30 DAYS?

☐ **YES**   ☐ NO

IF NO, CALL BACK OR SEND ANOTHER LETTER FOR IMMEDIATE REMOVAL.

IF YES, REVIEW INFORMATION AND EXAMINE TO MAKE SURE IT IS YOURS. IF NOT YOURS GO BACK TO DISPUTE STEPS AND FRAUD.

IF CALLED

SPOKE WITH _____

TIME _____ AM PM

DURING LISTEN DID THEY...

☐ STATE MINI-MIRANDA?

☐ VERIFY YOU?

IF THE DEBT COLLECTOR DID NOT DO EITHER OF THOSE STEPS PRIOR TO SPEAKING ABOUT YOUR DEBT, HANG UP, REPORT IT TO CFPB, FTC

Past Due Accounts: Collections

 DO NOT ADMIT TO THE DEBT

ACCOUNT/CREDITOR _____

ORIGINAL CREDITOR _____

REMOVAL DATE _____ / _____ / _____

☐ REQUEST VALIDATION

DATE _____ / _____ / _____

☐ FLAT RATE MAIL

☐ CALLED ➡

DID YOU RECEIVE VALIDATION WITHIN 30 DAYS?

☐ **YES**   ☐ **NO**

IF NO, CALL BACK OR SEND ANOTHER LETTER FOR IMMEDIATE REMOVAL.

IF YES, REVIEW INFORMATION AND EXAMINE TO MAKE SURE IT IS YOURS. IF NOT YOURS GO BACK TO DISPUTE STEPS AND FRAUD.

IF CALLED

SPOKE WITH _____

TIME _____ AM PM

DURING LISTEN DID THEY...

☐ STATE MINI-MIRANDA?

☐ VERIFY YOU?

IF THE DEBT COLLECTOR DID NOT DO EITHER OF THOSE STEPS PRIOR TO SPEAKING ABOUT YOUR DEBT, HANG UP, REPORT IT TO CFPB, FTC

Past Due Accounts: Collections

 DO NOT ADMIT TO THE DEBT

ACCOUNT/CREDITOR _____

ORIGINAL CREDITOR _____

REMOVAL DATE _____ / _____ / _____

☐ REQUEST VALIDATION

DATE _____ / _____ / _____

☐ FLAT RATE MAIL

☐ CALLED ➡️

DID YOU RECEIVE VALIDATION WITHIN 30 DAYS?

☐ **YES**   ☐ **NO**

IF NO, CALL BACK OR SEND ANOTHER LETTER FOR IMMEDIATE REMOVAL.

IF YES, REVIEW INFORMATION AND EXAMINE TO MAKE SURE IT IS YOURS. IF NOT YOURS GO BACK TO DISPUTE STEPS AND FRAUD.

IF CALLED

SPOKE WITH _____

TIME _____ AM PM

DURING LISTEN DID THEY...

☐ STATE MINI-MIRANDA?

☐ VERIFY YOU?

IF THE DEBT COLLECTOR DID NOT DO EITHER OF THOSE STEPS PRIOR TO SPEAKING ABOUT YOUR DEBT, HANG UP, REPORT IT TO CFPB, FTC

Past Due Accounts: Collections

 DO NOT ADMIT TO THE DEBT

ACCOUNT/CREDITOR _____

ORIGINAL CREDITOR _____

REMOVAL DATE _____ / _____ / _____

☐ REQUEST VALIDATION

DATE _____ / _____ / _____

☐ FLAT RATE MAIL

☐ CALLED ➡

DID YOU RECEIVE VALIDATION WITHIN 30 DAYS?

☐ **YES**   ☐ NO

IF NO, CALL BACK OR SEND ANOTHER LETTER FOR IMMEDIATE REMOVAL.

IF YES, REVIEW INFORMATION AND XAMINE TO MAKE SURE IT IS YOURS. IF NOT YOURS GO BACK TO DISPUTE STEPS AND FRAUD.

IF CALLED

SPOKE WITH _____

TIME _____ AM
PM

DURING LISTEN
DID THEY...

☐ STATE MINI-MIRANDA?

☐ VERIFY YOU?

IF THE DEBT COLLECTOR DID NOT DO EITHER OF THOSE STEPS PRIOR TO SPEAKING ABOUT YOUR DEBT, HANG UP, REPORT IT TO CFPB, FTC

Past Due Accounts: Collections

 DO NOT ADMIT TO THE DEBT

ACCOUNT/CREDITOR _____

ORIGINAL CREDITOR _____

REMOVAL DATE _____ / _____ / _____

☐ REQUEST VALIDATION

DATE _____ / _____ / _____

☐ FLAT RATE MAIL

☐ CALLED ➡

DID YOU RECEIVE VALIDATION WITHIN 30 DAYS?

☐ **YES**   ☐ NO

IF NO, CALL BACK OR SEND ANOTHER LETTER FOR IMMEDIATE REMOVAL.

IF YES, REVIEW INFORMATION AND EXAMINE TO MAKE SURE IT IS YOURS. IF NOT YOURS GO BACK TO DISPUTE STEPS AND FRAUD.

IF CALLED

SPOKE WITH _____

TIME _____ AM PM

DURING LISTEN DID THEY...

☐ STATE MINI-MIRANDA?

☐ VERIFY YOU?

IF THE DEBT COLLECTOR DID NOT DO EITHER OF THOSE STEPS PRIOR TO SPEAKING ABOUT YOUR DEBT, HANG UP, REPORT IT TO CFPB, FTC

Past Due Accounts: Collections

 DO NOT ADMIT TO THE DEBT

ACCOUNT/CREDITOR _____

ORIGINAL CREDITOR _____

REMOVAL DATE ___ / ___ / ___

☐ REQUEST VALIDATION

DATE ___ / ___ / ___

☐ FLAT RATE MAIL

☐ CALLED ➡

DID YOU RECEIVE VALIDATION WITHIN 30 DAYS?

☐ **YES**   ☐ NO

IF NO, CALL BACK OR SEND ANOTHER LETTER FOR IMMEDIATE REMOVAL.

IF YES, REVIEW INFORMATION AND EXAMINE TO MAKE SURE IT IS YOURS. IF NOT YOURS GO BACK TO DISPUTE STEPS AND FRAUD.

IF CALLED

SPOKE WITH _____

TIME _____ AM
PM

DURING LISTEN DID THEY...

☐ STATE MINI-MIRANDA?

☐ VERIFY YOU?

IF THE DEBT COLLECTOR DID NOT DO EITHER OF THOSE STEPS PRIOR TO SPEAKING ABOUT YOUR DEBT, HANG UP, REPORT IT TO CFPB, FTC

References

More information & Bonus Material

Dispute Letter package

I discontinued my credit repair services in 2022 but still want to offer this great DIY package for you. This package includes 8 dispute letters, 2 ebooks, and an informational sheet, as well as a video from me providing best practices. The two strategy ebooks are for Vehicle repossession and Bankruptcy removal. Dispute letter templates included are:

- Late payment removal
- Hard Inquiry Removal
- Personal Information incorrect
- Validation Request
- Failed to validate
- Method of Verification
- Reinsertion letter
- Settlement-pay-to-delete

Since you purchased this book or package you get an additional $5 off my dispute letter template package. Enter **promo code TAKE5** at checkout. Once purchased, you will immediately receive a link to download your digital product, along with an emailed link that will last for 30 days. Scan the QR Code or go to https://www.lisesbusiness.com/product-page/Dispute-letter-templates.

Laws and Regulators

The Federal Trade Commission (FTC) enforces a variety of antitrust and consumer protection laws affecting virtually every area of commerce. The FTC enforces the Fair Debt Collection Practices Act (FDCPA), which makes it illegal for debt collectors to use abusive, unfair, or deceptive practices when they collect debts.

The Fair Debt Collection Practices Act (FDCPA) (15 USC 1692 et seq.), which became effective in March 1978, was designed to eliminate abusive, deceptive, and unfair debt collection practices.

The Fair Credit Reporting Act (FCRA) is a federal law that helps to ensure the accuracy, fairness, and privacy of the information in consumer credit bureau files. The law regulates the way credit reporting agencies can collect, access, use and share the data they collect in your consumer reports.

The Consumer Financial Protection Bureau (CFPB) was created to provide a single point of accountability for enforcing federal consumer financial laws and protecting consumers in the financial marketplace. Have supervisory authority over banks, thrifts, and credit unions with assets over $10 billion, as well as their affiliates. Have supervisory authority over nonbank mortgage originators and servicers, payday lenders, and private student lenders of all sizes.

Reasons Your Credit Scores Can Fluctuate

- Utilization Increased - The balances on your accounts affect your score by as much as 30% If balances increase, in some cases even by just a little bit your score can drop.
- Reduced Credit Lines - Creditors periodically check your credit report by a soft check. They check to see how you're doing with your other accounts. If they see you have new negative credit or your utilization is too high, they may reduce your credit line and that can increase your utilization and in turn, decrease your score.
- New Credit / Inquiries - If you apply for credit, it will typically leave an inquiry on your report which will lower your score.
- New Collections, Public Records, or Late Payments - If new negative items hit your report, the score will decline.
- Status Changes - The status of specific accounts holds weight on your score. If a creditor charges off an account that can impact the score. Another possible reason is if you make a payment on an old collection account, which could re-age the account and change the status.

STATUTE OF LIMITATIONS ON DEBT

The statute of limitations in the case of debt refers to how long the creditor or collector has to take legal action against you. **This is different from the length of time a debt remains on your credit report.** The creditor cannot file a valid lawsuit outside of the statute of limitations. That means that they cannot use legal remedies, such as judgments, liens, and garnishments, to collect from you if the statute of limitations has passed.

STATE	ORAL	WRITTEN	PROMISSORY	OPEN
ALABAMA	6	6	6	3
ALASKA	3	3	3	3
ARIZONA	3	6	6	3
ARKANSAS	3	5	3	3
CALIFORNIA	2	4	4	4
COLORADO	6	6	6	6
CONNECTICUT	3	6	6	3
DELAWARE	3	3	3	4
FLORIDA	4	5	5	4
GEORGIA	4	6	6	6
HAWAII	6	6	6	6
IDAHO	4	5	5	5
ILLINOIS	5	10	10	5
INDIANA	6	6	10	6
IOWA	5	10	5	5
KANSAS	3	5	5	3
KENTUCKY	5	10	15	5
LOUISIANA	10	10	10	3

MAINE	6	6	6	6
MARYLAND	3	3	6	3
MASSACHUSETTS	6	6	6	6
MICHIGAN	6	6	6	6
MINNESOTA	6	6	6	6
MISSISSIPPI	3	3	3	3
MISSOURI	5	10	10	5
MONTANA	5	8	8	5
NEBRASKA	4	5	5	4
NEVADA	4	6	3	4
NEW HAMPSHIRE	3	3	6	3
NEW JERSEY	6	6	6	6
NEW MEXICO	4	6	6	4
NEW YORK	6	6	6	6
NORTH CAROLINA	3	3	5	3
NORTH DAKOTA	6	6	6	6
OHIO	6	8	15	6
OKLAHOMA	3	5	5	3
OREGON	6	6	6	6
PENNSYLVANIA	4	4	4	4
RHODE ISLAND	10	10	10	10
SOUTH CAROLINA	3	3	3	3
SOUTH DAKOTA	6	6	6	6
TENNESSEE	6	6	6	6

TEXAS	4	4	4	4
UTAH	4	6	6	4
VERMONT	6	6	5	3
VIRGINIA	3	5	6	3
WASHINGTON	3	6	6	3
WEST VIRGINIA	5	10	6	5
WISCONSIN	6	6	10	6
WYOMING	8	10	10	8

Debt Collection Practices

- Debt Collectors or collections can only call between 8 a.m. to 9 p.m.
- Debt collectors may not harass you or anyone else, over the phone or through any other form of contact when collecting on a debt.
- If your employer does not allow you to receive personal calls at work, you should let the debt collector know that.
- If you chose to speak with them, they must verify they are speaking with the correct person. They may ask you, for instance, "is this Charlise Rice that I am speaking to?", just to make sure they have the right person to the debt. Also, they will verify the last four of your social security number too.
- Debt Collection agencies are required to state the Mini-Miranda. Must state, "This is an attempt to collect a debt and any information obtained will be used for that purpose".

BONUS MATERIAL

SUPPLEMENTARY REPORTS

According to the CFPB, Consumer Reporting Companies collect information and provide reports to other companies about you. These companies use these reports to inform decisions about providing you with credit, employment, residential rental housing, insurance, and in other decision-making situations. There are hundreds of them!! We are going to focus on the larger ones that CFPB refers to as Supplementary Reports. Supplementary Reports are information that some consumer reporting companies sell and are used to supplement other data, such as the credit data the nationwide consumer reporting companies sell about you. This information can include public records and ID verification data to help firms manage credit and fraud risks. LexisNexis, Innovis, and CoreLogic Credco are the largest data aggregators of supplementary reports. You can opt out and or place a security freeze.

Do not hesitate to look at other types of consumer reporting companies listed on the CFPB website to check what data is available and if you can opt-out or request a security freeze. https://www.consumerfinance.gov/consumer-tools/credit-reports-and-scores/consumer-reporting-companies/companies-list/

LexisNexis

LexisNexis reports data such as real estate ownership, lien, judgment, bankruptcy records, professional license information, motor vehicle reports, and historical addresses. You can obtain a copy of your consumer disclosure report, request to opt-out and place a security freeze.

- Request a copy of your consumer disclosure credit report https://consumer.risk.lexisnexis.com/consumer
- Opt-out form: https://optout.lexisnexis.com/. Select - I do not want my information available for distribution to the general public. The opt-out process can take up to 30 days for it to take effect.
- Security Freeze: Call LexisNexis consumer center at 888-497-0011. Inform them that you want to place a security freeze on your account. The freeze will take effect in 3 three business days.

Innovis

Innovis is another Credit Reporting Bureau. Innovis is not as major as Equifax, TransUnion, and Experian. You can do a credit check with Innovis and receive a copy of their credit report, but that is not their primary service. For the most part, Innovis deals directly with businesses to authenticate consumer data, sometimes for use in pre-approved credit and insurance offers. One thing that Innovis does not provide that the other credit bureaus do is a credit score. You can request your credit report and place a security freeze online.

- Request a copy of your credit report online. https://www.innovis.com/creditReport/index
- Security Freeze: https://www.innovis.com/personal/securityFreeze

CORELOGIC CREDCO

CoreLogic Credco is a major provider of merged credit reports to mortgage lenders and dealerships. You can request a credit report and security freeze on their website.

https://www.corelogic.com/support/teletrack-consumer-assistance/

- Credit report- Fill out and mail the consumer request form. Complete the form and either mail or fax it to them. You must include a copy of your government-issued identification card (for example, a Driver's License) containing your address. If your current address is different from that stated on your government-issued identification card, you must provide either a utility bill, cell phone bill, cable bill, or military orders. Your current address has to be on the document you are going to provide.
- Security Freeze: Request security Freeze via Teletrack secure link. They will respond via email with a secure link. You will have to fill out a form, sign it and reply with a copy of your government-issued identification card and current utility bill. You may also request a security freeze on your file by contacting them at 877-309-5226 or faxing at 800-237-6526.

NOTES

_____

_____

_____

_____

_____

_____

_____

_____

_____

_____

_____

NOTES

_____

_____

_____

_____

_____

_____

_____

_____

_____

_____

NOTES

NOTES

_____

_____

_____

_____

_____

_____

_____

_____

_____

_____

_____

Lise's Business Enterprise

Professional Resource Consultant

www.LisesBusiness.com

Info@lisesBusiness.com